The Underlook

The Underlook

Helen Seymour

smith|doorstop

the poetry business

Published 2022 by The Poetry Business
Campo House,
54 Campo Lane,
Sheffield S1 2EG
www.poetrybusiness.co.uk

Copyright © Helen Seymour 2022
The moral rights of the author have been asserted.
ISBN 978-1-914914-00-3
eBook ISBN 978-1-914914-01-0

Designed & typeset by The Poetry Business.
Printed by Imprint Digital.

British Library Cataloguing-in-Publication Data.
A catalogue record for this book is available from the British Library.

Smith|Doorstop is a member of Inpress
www.inpressbooks.co.uk.
Distributed by IPS UK, 1 Deltic Avenue,
Rooksley, Milton Keynes MK13 8LD.

The Poetry Business gratefully acknowledges the support
of Arts Council England.

Supported using public funding by
ARTS COUNCIL
ENGLAND

Although the body was that of a dog, Possum's head was made of wax and shaped like a human's, and I could not have wished for a more convincing likeness.
– Matthew Holness, *Possum*

Contents

Child Development Centre 1996

Helen is starting to break her falls by putting out her arms. She's had three episodes in which she has cried because of her hands; she says that they don't hurt but is obviously uncomfortable. Helen is very shy in the clinic, and I hear very little speech. I understand that the content of her speech is normal but strangers have some difficulty understanding her.

Crack

She got drenched in blue staccato
at four in the morning.
Bit on the mouthpiece and sucked,
chucked up beige in the back of the sick bus,
ambulance yellow and green paramedics –
it's all nausea to me.

Surgery was white dust and blood,
she was all they talked about over taps and the nail brush:
a girl had tried to plaster cast her heart
and by the looks of what they pulled out
it only half-worked.

'She'll be disappointed'
one of them said.
Six hours later her bed was empty.
She was found wandering round the fracture clinic,
falling in love with broken people.

Pumped up with morphine, back into bed,
by nightfall they found her
making chains with her intestines.
The sheets were blood and brown and black,
the moon was a cut
and her stitches were embedded, deep.

Next to each other by the sinks again,
turned the tap down to make sure he was heard:
'Told you she'd be gutted.'
The other one laughed and had to wash his hands,
this time, because of the spit.

Beep

The anaesthetist I've been dating is really starting
to annoy me, not once has he told me that I've still
got some of the general anaesthetic left in me
and it's very rare but it *can* stay in you for this long,
but as a special treat tonight, he'll take me
to the hospital, beep us into an empty room,
I'll lie down and he'll put suction cups
over each part of my face and drain it from me,
it will be black and thick, he'll pour
it into a see-through plastic bag, clip the top
and put it in the medical waste bin, clean my face
with a cold wet wipe, and tell me, soon, I'll be awake.

Heaving

Every time I see you, I vomit,
and you see it, the beige-but-not-
boring gloop of tea and saliva and
yeast and satsuma. You never
mention it, not anymore, you just
look away while I take the kitchen
roll and wipes I carry around with me
and do my best to clean it up, clean
it off me. Try and save the train
ticket I bought just to see you.
We carry on walking, whether
it be over a bridge in London
or from your hallway to your lounge.
If you leave the room and come
back into it I'm sick again,
all over myself. I think back
to the time you didn't ignore it –
the first time it happened –
when you helped take off my
clothes. The gentleness
of your hands, slowly sliding the cotton
above me. All I wanted to do was
run your cotton above you
and breathe in the smell of your neck
but of course, it wasn't that.
Not at all. I knew that it had never
crossed your mind, as though, to you,
I wasn't even a woman, but some animal
you were fond of. The first day
I threw up in front of you, you looked
at me like I was trapped in a snare,
whispering, 'hey there lil' bunny,'

as you dabbed me softly
with white wool, 'let's get you
cleaned up and on your way home.'

Psychic

My first and only visit to a psychic
cost me twenty-five pounds and took
place in a pub on the outskirts
of Herne Bay. I wore the plainest
clothes I owned and didn't do my hair
or my eyeliner so she couldn't
cold read me. The minute I sat
down, she asked me if my dad's
dad was dead. Actually, she asked
whether he 'was in spirit?' It took
me a second
to say yes and then she smiled,
and told me that he
says *hello*.
She didn't bring him up again,
moved on to saying I'd fallen
into the wrong career and need to fall
out of it. 'Hello,' I thought, walking home,
I mean can you really believe it?
That's her message for me, from 'spirit'.
From long-in-the-ground-grandpa.
Hel-fucking-lo. You know, I shouted
the word the rest of my way
to my front door HELLO
HELLO HELLLOOOO! HELLLOOOOOOOOO-
O-O-O-O-O-O into the shadowed
supermarkets and the pitch black
swimming pool HELLO
HELLLOOOO HELLO at the stock-still
swings and the empty benches
and the bodies in pyjamas
from behind the double glaze.

14

[Rearranging the words of]
Case Dismissed in Slaying of Deformed Baby

LA Times *article, July 14th 1990, from Associated Press*

A baby broke into a delivery room and said 'there will be no
more practices.' In one ecstatic motion, he snuffed out the
floor. But moments after that, it returned. Fingers tried to be
infant, life cleft on a technicality. The veterinary wife moved
into a point, into tears of twice and two. She absolutely had
both in there. Murder juries the judge, judge judges the
court, clients, the veterinarian, her attorney for his assistant
attorney, the state, his states, to state, of in case, charges, the
proceedings, the juries, the boy. His attorney met the years
in defence. Said who did, to that, said who said, contended
this, on a not, argued at, been made to, dismissed when,
have left. Done. Slammed one, slammed seven. Bring in a
realizing. Murder appealed the murder. Sustain. Trial the
trials. The insanity born in that terrible final state, that had
driven on, ruling with the delivery. The charge charges
after the evidence. Argued the condition was on trial.
Dismissal over. An ago granted. The son cannot deserve
a lesser state. Excuse medicine hung child against palate.
Ended appeals webbed on the floor. Deformities did not
judge. His attorney defects. The south creature hung on his
slaying circuit, killing charge. His new-born son was not a
temporary child. He had not deserved such a horrible 'after'.
The suburb ruled. The room was enough. Charge against a
fate of dismissal. It's the boy against his birth.

Spinal Fusion

The patient will click the shutter with the lens covered
The patient will spend hours staring at flecks in the carpet
The patient will soak stains in boiling water
The patient will daydream about lichen
The patient will write 'arm' on her arm
The patient will clean extracted teeth
The patient will draw cardiograms in white crayon
The patient will Sellotape the door closed
The patient will pin books to the ceiling
The patient will acrylic the television screen
The patient will cut bread with a cocktail stick
The patient will plaster the floor
The patient will enter closed competitions
The patient will catch insects to bring inside
The patient will throw keys onto the roof
The patient will buy candles but no matches
The patient will dictate the rain
The patient will paint the underside of her nails
The patient will wear a seatbelt without driving
The patient will seal the showerhead
The patient will get dressed at 4am
The patient will tug at automatic doors
The patient will plan in old calendars
The patient will push her post back through the letterbox
The patient will hide money on the pavement
The patient will dial her own number
The patient will build a treehouse at the root
The patient will inhale balloons
The patient will jump onto diving boards

The patient will drag sticks into the lane
The patient will sleep on the roof of an ambulance
The patient will pull the emergency cord
The patient will climb up it like steps, like a ladder
The patient will feel it tightening in the dark

You're Just So Funny I Can't Stop Laughing

rocking backwards, my head
bumps the coffee table and this
shuddering accident revives the tiny
shrieks till a deep breath breaks,
in no time I'm tripped back
toward the table, the corner pushes
on the same spot, my hands walk
me forward, mouth trembling I reach
for my tea on the slate coaster, concentrate
my tongue on the chipped rim – swallow – oh god,
my lips repel like magnets and my head knocks rigid
again hahahahahaahaaaa a second, third, fourth
mouth opens inside my torso like
coat buttons, like a stone skimming, my head hits
twice as hard this time it's broken the skin and
the coffee table turns scarlet – whatever ghost
inside is fitting, epileptic and when
the glass tears through to bone the sound
changes from hard and high to soft and
mush – I'm blind for the briefest second
still I'm shaking out half-words, opened
like the hatch to an attic, peeling
back roof tiles, breaking through clouds,
heading beyond oxygen,
surrender the radars, abandon the trackers, rescue is futile

The Wasp in Room Ten

She flew in and landed on me,
looking to scavenge.
I screamed but the sound
came out of the wound.
She heard it like apple juice,
crawling towards the bandages,
ready to burrow in and collect.
I called for hands to tweezer
her out but they just rested on
the metal frame and left.
I could feel her body threatening
to disconnect as she worked,
gathering my stitches to use
as legs for her children.

24 Hours in A&E

Lillian

The episode blurb says, 'Lillian is brought in after being accidentally run over by her husband.' The doctors ask her, 'How bad is your pain out of ten?' She says nine, you have to say nine; if you say ten, they think you're being over-dramatic. If you say eight or less, they think it can't be that bad. They are having to pull her out of the scanner because her blood pressure is very low and it's setting off an alarm. They say her heart looks 'unremarkable.'

Peter

Richard's wife woke up to him having a seizure. A doctor scrawls over the lines of an answer box while a porter tilts on a black office chair. Peter is wheeled in. Another wife wakes in the night and walks into the hall, blood all down the stairs, until she finds her husband in the spare room, covered and oh my god there he is – yep, utterly covered. The paramedic says, in a fairly jolly tone, '... this is Peter, he's 57, and his wife found him unconscious and blood soaked,' like it's an episode of blind date. Blood all over the house, the lounge, the stairs, the hall, the bed. Richard has another seizure as he slides into the MRI and now his wife is talking to the camera about how they met. 'The air would fizz around him.' The seizure passes and he manages to show the doctor his tongue. A part of me expects the nurse to place a Parma Violet on it.

Fiona

The phone is ringing and Fiona is going straight to CT: she is 80 and fell backwards into an empty swimming pool. She rang her son and said, 'Richard, I think I'm hurt.' The doctor said, 'The height she fell?' The paramedic said, 'Three metres,' and the doctor went, 'Three ...' and then did a double take, 'THREE metres?' They've just edited in her son, talking after the event, 'I wanted them to put Savlon on her head but it didn't work out like that.' She is covered in bubble wrap. They've cut in a shot of the swimming pool when it was first built, in black and white, like when you see a photograph of a serial killer as a child.

Jenny

A doctor warns another doctor, 'A horse can cause internal injuries that you can't always see,' as though Jenny has swallowed one. There is no obvious injury but she's letting out tiny cries. Vinny is wheeled in, holding a blood-stained bucket. He's had a three-hour nose bleed and it's all down his pyjamas. I think they chose to show Vinny because Vinny *looks* like he's been kicked by a horse. Jenny had to crawl to the other side of the field to flag down a car. A cleaner just carried a drenched mop from right to left and back again. Jenny's pelvis is shattered – she's worried about her dog business. She says no one took her seriously when she wanted to be a dog-walker full time.

James

Pam's struggling to concentrate. The first thing she says to the nurse is, 'I came by helicopter.' A packet of crisps has got stuck in the vending machine and at the back of the shot there's a paramedic with a blurred-out face; he either doesn't want to be filmed or that's just how his face is. The receptionists wear blouses with white spots on. James has crashed his motorbike: he has a spinal cord injury, an open fracture on his wrist and a dislocated pelvis. Meanwhile, the doctors talk Pam through her scan results; I think she can still hear propellers rotating in her head. An ambulance carefully reverses between two other ambulances. When James' wife arrives, they sit her down in the relatives' room to warn her it was a serious accident and seeing him might be a shock. Her tears leave a mark. No one ever warns the patients about how their relatives look.

Max

He said he heard a pop when it went in. Before they clean the blood off, they lever out the driftwood, dropping it into a Ziploc bag that the nurse is careful to close, running her fingers over the seal more than once.

Gordon

A nurse tells Gordon not to move his head; he stood on loose floorboards and plummeted onto concrete. He calls his wife – 'What happened?' – 'Nothing. I just fell over.' A plastic fish bobs in a long tube while a doctor talks about how good his telephone voice is. The camera zooms in on a grey number 3 on the floor. A toddler has hurt his eye

and he's refusing to show anyone. They try to distract him
with bubbles, but he can do bubbles one handed. A nurse
in blue gloves plugs a wire into Gordon. Number 6 on the
floor now. They tell him he's got fluid in his abdomen; he
says, 'Oh it could be ... because I've had some breakfast?' A
nurse puts cold jelly on his stomach. The toddler shoves the
bubble wand into the pot and mixes. Gordon throws up a
lot of black vomit and says, 'Right, is this serious, or ...?'

My Time in the Hospital

Mate, mate –
honestly –
I'm breathing with three lungs,
I've learnt a new taste,
noticed another number
on the face of my watch,
there's better lighting
in my dreams,
I can feel a new smoothness
to my teeth,
a new kick in my boots
I can see the other blue
in the sky now,
understand why ants
work in teams

Mate,
it was off the charts
I had a record player in my room
played slow hip hop
I danced, mate
I danced on the bed
the nurse moved it up and down
to the beat
like u-u-u-u-u-up
then do-o-o-o-ow-w-wwwn
when it dropped

I'm going to write a show
with costumes and a band –
mate, mate,
I'm going to paint watercolours

of the call button,
they will be the size of stamps
white canvas, tiny orange circle
thousands of them mate,
I can't wait to get started,
I'm going to find that fabric
they use for the gowns
recover my notebooks
my shoes
the handles of my cutlery

What's that?
no, no, they discharged me –
I'm headed home right now,
calling you from the car –
what?
no, mate, of course not –
it's a tin can –
I've got one hand on the wheel,
the window's open,
the string is tight,
and the other can
is trailing in the road

Subject: P.E., Form III, 2000

Helen is beginning to find it more and more difficult to keep up with her peers, but remains absolutely determined to keep trying and have a go at everything. She has made some improvements, particularly with her catching skills and her throwing, which is more accurate, although, unfortunately, lacks length.

Falling

was an untraceable shape,
the thwack was a noise you'll never repeat,
so say, instead, a prayer to the position
you have landed in: you are the antithesis
of what caught you, this is likely
one of the only times in your life
where you can fully appreciate
how soft a body can become,
feel how the heat rushes, swellings blushed
pink, blooming, prickling bones,
kiss your laggy arms, feel
the capillaries ooze, the joins detach,
the limpness and the privilege
to inhabit such blatant, living dud.

Fire Escape

Absolutely decked it down a fire escape,
didn't even need to evacuate;
there was no emergency, no smoke
creeping under the door,
no need to push the silver bar
and hurry down the zig-zagging steps.

I lay at the foot of the empty lighthouse
unable to move. For a while,
I let myself imagine
the head of a young girl peering
from the window of a low-flying plane.
Hypothetically, would I get a mention
in her vocal notes on the landscape?
Imagine not making the cut.

Insects began to clean themselves
on my stomach and eyelids while
I replayed the moment I spontaneously
smashed the 'BREAK GLASS IN CASE OF',
like a mantra in my aching head.

When the red engine came,
the white-light siren drowned out my voice
and the firemen stepped over my grappling,
screaming body in search of the blaze.

You're Looking Well

Along with my discharge notes, and instructions to stay bed-bound, I get a certificate. It is on ivory paper with a navy-blue embossed border. I get my mum to hang it above me. It says: 'Helen died on the operating table but we brought her back to life.' It is signed by a doctor and says MBBS next to her name. When people visit, I point to it with a large stick I ordered from the internet. Ninety percent of the time, people ask, 'Did you have an out-of-body experience?' Then there is a knock at the door. They answer it and it's the actual me: fully formed, flesh and opaque. She walks in and sits at the end of my bed. At this point the visitor usually drops their grapes. We say, 'yes,' in unison, watch them compare and wonder who'll be the first to speak.

*

Where is Hugo?

In 2019, a piglet named Hugo vanished. Hugo had been taken from a farm by a vegan vlogger who intended to raise him at home. But after the first night, Hugo was never seen again. Eventually, the vlogger agreed to an interview, in which he insisted Hugo was fine, but wouldn't say where he was or what happened. Everyone just left it there, with no explanation for why or how the piglet suddenly disappeared.

Missing

I designed some posters on Microsoft Word.
The word MISSING was in Cooper Black (bold).
I spent three hours on the colour wheel,
choosing just the right red (#EE381A).
Below the picture, in the same colour
and the same font, I wrote:
HE CAN'T HAVE JUST VANISHED
and my telephone number, and the police's
telephone number.

I asked Fiona at the Post Office to print
them off for me, and I've just come back
from picking them up. Her ink cartridge
started to get low halfway through the job.
Thin stripes of white run through the letters,
but she told me that she
didn't think it really mattered.

Back to the Scene

My car is pointing directly at the house.
The engine's running, headlights shining
into each shadowed window.
I follow every flicker in a quick,
restless search for activity:
a handle turning, a curtain quivering,
a change in the position of the kitchen tap:
anything, *anything*, beyond the small
black silhouettes dancing in my eyes.

Say They'd Taken It Seriously

The police are here.
They are dusting for tiny trotter marks.
A woman dressed in fragile white
searches for signs
of a bag being packed, a note.

They are waiting for reinforcements
to make a start on the garden.
No evidence of a tiny miniature cross made
from two lollipop sticks,
but there are four Mini Milks
in the freezer.

A call is made to the local slaughterhouse
to check for any voluntary admissions.
There is no Hugo on the register,
no suspicious post,
no threatening messages on the answerphone.
When a coolbox is found in the garage
they expect the worst,
but it's just potato smiley faces
and a medical ice pack, for sprains.

The team are told to leave all possibilities open:
he may have rolled himself into a pin-striped hammock,
be hiding in your grandmother's attic,
moonlighting in a Spanish laundrette.

He could be thousands of miles away,
or watching us at this very moment.
Look for a tiny piglet riding a ghost train;
we will lose this case the second
we forget he could be anywhere.

The Vicar Said I Need To Stop Searching For Hugo

so I called him a hypocrite and added his name to the list
of suspects.

Chase the Forest

I'm running blind through thick green
the next beat freezing dead, ears stretching
to a crackle in the leaves, branches snapping
or is the loudest thing my breath?
I'm second-guessing the silence, double
crossing my own trainers, drenched and unlaced

Somewhere my mother's voice is warning: 'unlaced!'
warning lights flashing, but I'm cold hard green
I'm seeing in fours and fives, half a day past double
the ground, the branches, the night is stretching
out then in close to me, trying to snatch my breath
and I'm shouting back at nothing, snapping

Using my gut as a fleshy compass, snapping
back and forth between feeling unlaced
and having this sewn up, together. My breath
expelling hazy ghosts against the green
I don't pause to watch but I know they're stretching
into nothing, stars pulse out, the moon's bent double

Running green through thick blind, the trees double
they're snapping, snap—I'm snapping,
whack the ground and feel my body stretching
out onto the muddy earth, like I'm roots, unlaced
ghosts are expelling me against the murky green,
lungs stutter in the rhythm of the in and the out breath

Can you really know your own breath?
Could you tell between yours and your double?
I can't even pretend this forest is green
anymore, the dark set in quickly, it's snapping

every colour out of sight, my mouth is unlaced
a guttural scream of a girl or a guttural girl stretching?

I'm coiled now, there's no stretching
left, my legs on empty, red light, breath
a flickering compass, my fleshy gut unlaced
I'm cold hard silence and trying to double
back the way I—hear a crunch, snapping
I'm sewn up, paused in the hidden green

I'm not going to leave this green yet, despite unlaced laces
stretching like a mouth for breath, I can double down, snapping
a long scream into hundreds of calls for the same, small name

Fever Dream

I'm suckling on the air valve of a bouncy castle,
breathing in the bumps. Shoes scatter
the ground but I can't find
a pair, every time I try to join the jumping
I deflate. A child pulls my arm
into a dark blue playhouse. An
old television connected to a plasticine
plug socket shows black and white
footage of a woman, trapped in a red
telephone box, banging on the glass,
rattling the door. It ends with her
giving in and picking up the call, before
looping back to the start. Butterfly arms,
front crawl legs, face of a girl who's just
lost her float. The same child who pulled me
in here circles the wooden hut on a
bright pink bicycle with flashing lights
on the handlebars. I try to catch her attention
but she can't hear me, and the door
is jammed shut. The TV remote
does nothing, no other channel, until
I realise I'm switching the child on the
bike to a man on the bike to a nurse on
the bike to a soldier on the bike,
a piglet on the bike, me
on the bike and I'm out and I'm free
I'm weaving through the shoes
round the empty castle and out
into fields pedalling faster and faster
before someone else flicks me
into nothing to see what's
on the other side.

*

Subject: English, Form II, 1999 (Exercise Book)

When I opened the door I found a bedroom. There was
a bed in the bedroom. A witch was in the bed. I was
frightened. The witch woke up. I ran down the stairs but she
caught me and put me in a dark room. She said she would
let me go in a hundred years but I escaped and ran home. I
locked the door behind me.

Adolescence

I moved into a well
at roughly eleven years old
became accustomed
to rugged rest and let
the murky water seek
a slow death on my skin
saw its dirt move upon me
let it settle under my nails
creep between my legs
and into my ears where
it nestled right beside
the drum and whispered
a rhythm – the dirt it
whispered – a rhythm
that tapped itself into
every part of me until
it was entrenched as deep
as teeth and eyes and legs
and arms entrenched dancing
to the same clockwork beat
that other girls hid
in streams of curved hips
and gushing

Parallel Universe

1am, New Year, lit only by the lights above the sink. I'm by the table, hand grasped to the wood for balance as my ankle boot misremembers my arches. I'm in the dark bit of the kitchen. Our friends fade into other rooms. The kettle is rose gold and they have a toaster with slots for four. I stamp my foot and the boot falls off completely. 'Fuck's sake, I got one on.' I'm looking at the dud shoe, waiting for you to laugh but you just step in-between me and it. I swallow. My laugh fragments into tiny breaths around my nose. The look in your eye holds me like the space beneath a hymn. You edge closer and your dark jacket and arms wrap around me. Your lips hesitate on the brink as I catch them. A smile splits in me and we talk on liquid mute. I slide up onto the table. We hear the others coming down the stairs. You whisper a joke about how you were just coming over to help me with my shoe. By the time the door handle presses down you've moved back and I'm fiddling with laces. Our friends have different names, blinds with shutters; they buy Hovis and still eat butter. I leave at quarter past, and sit for a while in my car, holding, as the year breaks itself open on something concrete.

Silver Shell Girl

At sixteen, I got a letter from the hospital
saying that I had to wear
a 14th century suit of armour
until further notice. There was a map attached,
with a location, date and time.
When I arrived, the woman
in the bridal shop hastily
took me to the back, where I waited
for thirty minutes on a high white stool.

She took my measurements
and said the metal would do me wonders,
excitedly showing me a range
of feather options for the helmet.
I rattled home, worried about the limited
roles I'd be offered in the school play.

Frequent trips to the toilets were needed
to oil myself, trying to stop the squeaking
that grew louder than my own voice.
On a history trip to a joust, I was nearly
arrested by a worried citizen when
they saw me board the school coach.
On the days spent leaning over a Bunsen
burner, heat shock nearly collapsed me.

I polished my torso with Vaseline
for the end of year disco,
and while the DJ spun Black Eyed Peas
(for the second time that night)
I spilt blackcurrant juice in the gap between
my body and the breastplate.

My friend and I stayed on the dancefloor
most of the night. We bumped to Flo Rida's
'Low', and there was quite
a sexy moment where I rode her
like a horse. Another mate told me
that one of the older boys,
that had gate-crashed from the pub,
kept looking at me, and I laughed,
gave him my number, then fantasized
ways to seize the hinges,
jam the mechanisms, and stay inside
my own clasps forever.

[Rearranging the Words of]
Parents Complain that Disabled TV Presenter is 'Scaring Children'

Evening Standard, *13th April 2012*

The Controller of Nightmares took the decision to hire me and dozens of mums, dads and children with disabilities last month. Ban all month-old quotas, we have a role every time. Can only be a good thing, a positive and important opportunity born from how scary minorities are in the day. We show children one arm and bedtime is disabled. Presenter one, presenter four and me message small comments over the big programme campaign.

Disturbing television is on: disability has children, a daughter, has a chance, will slot in, have as much love as conversations. Her natural father is disabled, wrote determination on her and she wrote it on her daughter. It goes on. A blogger thought disability his co-presenter, would give her warm boards, was solely with it, has complained to the upset talk. Difficult said 'the political' does that, but had to be even-minded, as he was prompted to entertain because he is of that employment. 'Their their,' comments said to the said said said.

So some children took the parents to meet at the General Board of Message Correctness. Others may have to channel one television to another, because of the using and because of the accused. Some think it's just about the show, and would ask who, just who, had removed the models? Who is prompted to? Anyone? What is it with that which?

Hiring new terrible woman to scare popular kids and their parents. Do the parent watching, children. Do it. Become or else. Discover that vicious channel think. Scaring millions, on at every available hour.

Mortuary

When I was a child, my brother and I would play The Tray Memory Game. You put objects on a tray, like string, a pencil, a playing card. It's key to have quite a few items. Then my brother would shut his eyes, I would remove one of the objects and he had to guess what had gone missing.

When I grew older, and found a job in the mortuary, I would play the same game with the pathologist. We didn't have to use a tray. He'd simply open the body and close his eyes. I would put whatever part I'd taken in the dark blue jar we kept next to the drill. I'd only return it once he had guessed correctly.

Previous surgeries, accidents and irregularities provided satisfying red herrings. When I seized an ear drum, he was totally distracted by the missing appendix. Another time, I took a nonagenarian's three remaining teeth, but the pathologist assumed she was toothless. He didn't get it until I shook the jar.

The afternoons passed quickly when we played the game. He said he liked trying to find what I'd taken more than trying to find the cause of death. I would often take small sips of Ribena while he searched.

After One Session of Therapy

I bungee-cord down
to a bridge builder
gauging the beams and say,
'Did your parents divorce?'

Sleep on the beach to catch
the early morning rise
of the local sand sculptor,
'Are you scared of commitment?'

Lean in to a cartographer
as they finish zig-zagging
on a mountain peak,
'Have you always felt lost?'

Crawl beneath the chair
of an aeroplane pilot
laddering atmosphere,
'Were you once bullied
by a very, very tall boy?'

Call a locksmith to the middle
of an empty, cropless field,
'Did your mother have a habit
of keeping secrets from you?'

Book an appointment with
a driving instructor, ten minutes
in tell them I can already drive, but
'do you tend to trust others
more than you trust yourself?'

Take a lilo out in choppy
oceans, watch the lifeguard
cut through waves to clutch me,
'Is part of you submerged?'

As her biro hovers, stare at the
tissue transcending the box,
'If you hit a deer while driving,
how far would you drag it
from the mark on the road?'

School Photographer

I sat down on the wooden box, sponge-blue background
behind me. The photographer said to drop my shoulders, sit
up straight, nice big smile. The flash swarmed my eyes. He
checked the picture. 'Sorry,' he said, 'let's try that again.' He
pressed the small black button and looked at the camera
screen. 'And … once more.' It went on, my shoulders
dropping less each time. Teachers, family and friends came
to get me but each time they saw the images, they agreed
it was worth another shot. The photographer stopped
apologising after a while. Weeks went by; my arms began to
warp and my feet broke the leather of my shoes. I forgot the
sounds I used to make, the ways I used to gather myself, to
stretch. I became a smoke alarm blaring from a blackened
bedsit, a brake light shining from the wreckage.

Witness Protection

The force of the wind here is making me
take trivial steps backwards, forwards,
and back again
as though on this very hillside I'm shuffling
on a miniature dance mat.

I took up the practice of standing
in bleak, deserted landscapes
in the hopes I may be the sole
witness to a particularly vicious crime.
I'm not aroused by violence, not a voyeur,
don't have an ounce of hero syndrome;
I've taken a diazepam and had two panic
attacks already. I jump at
the call of a pigeon.

I'm playing the long game here,
have been as soon as I heard
that, in witness protection,
you get a folder with all
the details of your new self,
and all the things you've ever done.

I tried making my own,
tried to pretend my whole existence
was dreamt up by an admin team,
tried to write instructions for myself in bold:
**DO NOT ELABORATE ON YOUR EXPERIENCES
IN THE ISLE OF WIGHT**,
but there I am, another dinner party,
another re-enactment of the crossing,
it'd be far easier if it was all an invention,

if I knew every detail of my life was made up,
certifiably faulty and incorrect,
not worth a second thought,
light enough to go in a folder.

Patient Care Documentation 2010

Evaluation: Observations stable. Scoring 1 on the mews due to tachycardia – 109 bpm. All other observations within normal limits. Taking sips of water regularly. IDC draining minimal amounts of urine. Vomiting in the evening after taking Ondansetron and Oxynorm. Cyclizine given to good effect. Additional information: Helen said that she gets scared when the nurses come into her room to check her overnight

Postman Pat on Oxycontin

Pat is driving in his van
but he's got a little bit lost!
He gets out and has a walk around,
leaving the engine running.

Pat reads an address out loud,
he asks where that could be?
When no one answers, he posts it
into his open mouth.

Pat is sick in the pond!
He watches as the fish
ignore his foaming insides
and sink back down to the bottom.

Pat covers his face, as though
he is playing hide and seek
but instead of numbers
he repeatedly shouts his own name.

Pat tries to dig himself
a new home in the dirt
since he can't remember where he lives
and is scared of his son's round head.

Pat curls into a ball and chews
his thumb until it tears.
When no blood appears,
he presses his eye to the hole
as though he is a telescope
trying to focus
on a blinking light.

[Rearranging the Words of]
The Ethicist's Response to 'Is It OK to Dump Him Because of His Medical Condition?'

New York Times *column answering 'Ethical Quandaries',*
Published June 9, 2020

Once you have a spouse, you become seriously ill. Accept
it. You range your lives together, committing to deplorable
severity and enter the controlled condition of a debilitating
life. A specific mention of this relationship would make
someone consider what's truly meant by *the one*. That is, to
be unable to be you. Seriously, you make commitment think
it can't be committing. You enter a lover into a terrible
promise to think about – saying *that's that* and *this is it* –
marriage didn't or doesn't owe it to anyone to endure the
issue of a long life. She has all kinds of responsibilities before
you. If, for the may well, or would but when, to the then
would, to for, into it has, and to genuinely have. Partnership
is a burden, not such a mild term. Don't have potential,
don't be a person example, a before partner. Because indeed,
to like them is to be ill already. So, keep a friend or caregiver
as a good reason to abandon the person. Appropriately part
in health, because sickness can turn out to be someone you
can keep. He can be a course in precisely what you want.
You wide, terrible thing.

Lighter Fluid

My grandmother got trapped
in a jumper three days after giving birth
and, as soon as she was free
from the tight maroon, she ran
to the eaves of a Perspex bus shelter,
where I, although not born yet,
had been sitting for hours.

I was a teenager, in that cheap
shatter-proof hut,
chewing the end of a cigarette
that, in this life, I could never touch,
when my grandmother or – to me –
the young woman having a panic
attack, offered me a lighter.

The young woman screamed
as I intentionally set my hair ablaze,
telling her to relax; I was cold
and had no coat. She declined
to mention why she was only
wearing a skirt and bra; my scalp
was too blistered to ask.

In the end, I walked her back
to her house, my head a bleeding
lantern against her crowded sobs.
I extinguished when she slept,
and fell ahead in time, until
the hallowed voice of the bus driver
approached my unmade ear.

Well This Is Awkward

I'm going to do it.
I'm going to fucking do it.
Look – I've taken my shoes and socks off.
That's fucking serious.
And look.
Look at what I'm doing.
I am putting the note in my shoe.
My right,
no, my left,
yes, that's where I want it –
in my left shoe.
Right, in I go,
I am going in,
I am going,
I am going into the water.

Arggghhhh my foo—
bloody—that was a sharp
a very sharp pebble,
up to the ribs now,
I'm just going to wait,
wait here now,
just for a minute,
I sort of need a shit,
should I just ...?
I think it might mar the feeling
of euphoria I read about,
for me, anyway,
should I just shit in the sea?
But what if it chases me?
Oh you are kidding me.
Who the fuck is ...?

It's five in the morning,
why the fuck is he in the sea?

Oh Jesus he's seen me –
don't tell me he's—
oh fucking hell he's waving,
right, yeah
HIYA
don'tcomeoverdon'tcomeoverdon'tcome

he's wading over
I can't fucking believe this.

Where did he put *his* shoes then?
Oh he's still wearing his shoes,
should I be wearing mine?
I don't know why I took them off,
I think I just wanted somewhere to put the note.
Where did he put *his* note?
Ah, under a rock in the carpark.
Oh my god.
Oh my fucking god.
They're going to think we did this together.
Like a pact.

No one will believe we're strangers.
We'll be next to each other in the paper,
there'll be a complicated inquest,
what if they bury us together?
I wouldn't like that.
I've only ever had a single bed.
I'm going to wade back,
to put a P.S. on my note, explaining

okay, okay, okay – pen –
'... just a coincidence about the other guy,
having the same idea as I did'
and then –
I've still got space at the bottom –
is that okay?
Do I need to sign it again
to prove it was me?
Should I have written more?
Drawn a picture?
No, not a picture, that's—
although, should I put another kiss?
I've only put one kiss,
will that be enough?
I should re-read it, to check—
shit, I've made a few spelling mistakes,
shall I cross them out?
Will they know what I meant?

What I Actually Want To Do

is listen
to an American stranger
singing about his depression
for an hour, on repeat, next-
door's hoover
will hum from the 17th minute,
gently knocking
at the skirting board
on the adjoining wall and on
the line about
the world being wide
I will crouch down
to press my hand against
the white gloss shuddering

Acknowledgements and Notes

The quotation at the beginning of this book is from a short story by Matthew Holness called 'Possum', published in *Dead Funny: Horror Stories by Comedians* edited by Robin Ince and Johnny Mains (Salt, 2014).

In 'What I Actually Want to Do', the quoted song lyric about 'the world being wide' is from 'Adam's Song' by Blink-182 (1999).

In case of any doubt, the three articles used for the 'Rearranging' poems are genuine. Excluding names and one instance of a derogatory term for a cleft lip, I rearranged all the words to create the poems. The original articles can be found here:

'Case Dismissed in Slaying of Deformed Baby', *LA Times* Archives, July 14th, 1990, from Associated Press

'Is it OK to Dump Him Because of His Medical Condition?', The Ethicist Column by Kwame Anthony Appiah, *New York Times Magazine*, June 9th 2020

'Parents Complain that Disabled TV Presenter is Scaring Their Children', Ellen Widdup, *Evening Standard*, 13th April 2012

Thank you to <u>disability-memorial.org</u>, an archive of remembrance for disabled people who have been murdered by their families. This is where I found the story of a father who walked free after being charged with the murder of his newborn son. After seeing that his baby had syndactyly, cleft lip and cleft palate, he threw him on the floor of the delivery room. I could find no record of the newborn's first name but please know this whole book is for you. Rest in Peace, in Power, and beyond the hands that didn't know your worth.

Thank you to the disability activists on Instagram who first made me aware of the response from 'The Ethicist' (Kwame Anthony Appiah, a 'moral agony aunt' for the *NY Times*) to the question 'Is it OK to Dump Him Because of His Medical Condition?'. In short, The Ethicist indicated that dating someone with Chrohn's disease could be a burden and so it's OK to end the relationship. After heavy criticism, an addendum was added after the original response, expressing regret. Equal thanks to the criticism levelled at those complaining that Cerrie Burnell, a CBBC presenter with limb difference, was 'scaring their children'. All solidarity to Cerrie.

Thanks to Channel 4 for *24 Hours in A&E* and *How to Steal Pigs and Influence People*, two documentary programmes that provided inspiration for some of these poems.

Thank you to The Emma Press and Creative Future for publishing early versions of 'Beep' and 'Crack' in *The Emma Press Anthology of Illness* and *Important Nothings: Creative Future Literary Award Winners* respectively. Thanks to Arts Council England for providing DYCP funding to research and create this collection with mentorship from Caroline Bird. Thank you Caroline, not least for politely nodding along while I told you about my ideas for a series of poems about the Lion King on ketamine. Thank you Suzannah Evans, Gboyega Odubanjo, Katie McLean and everyone at The Poetry Business for having faith in me and this collection, it means more than you could ever know. Thank you to everyone involved in the Canterbury poetry scene, Apples and Snakes and Hannah Silva for believing in me from the very beginning and continuing to support me to this day.

Thank you to the night nurse who sat with me during one of the worst nights of my life after spinal surgery, gently telling me a story about a new camera he was bidding for on Ebay. I wanted to write you a poem but none of them were good enough for you. I've never forgotten your kindness, patience and empathy.

I am getting palpitations at the idea of listing friends and family in case I accidentally leave someone out. Special mention to my mum, though, because she is the strongest, most amazing person I know. Everybody else, all I can say is: know who you are, how much I love you, and that if I forgot you, the guilt would ruin this whole book for me. And finally, thanks to my little, twisted rogue of a duplicated bit of a chromosome for refusing to follow the rules.

www.helenseymour.com